Contents

Introduction 2
Chapter 1 - First Things First 4
Chapter 2 – Drug Crimes in Brief 7
Chapter 3 – The First Rung of the Ladder 9
Chapter 4 – Informant Development 13
Chapter 5 – Surveillance Tactics 19
Chapter 6 – Drug Operations 24
Chapter 7 – Consent searches 30
Chapter 8 – Moving Up the Ladder 32
Chapter 9 – Cash and Asset Seizures 34
Chapter 10 – They Lie, But You Can't 36
Chapter 11 – Some Things Narcs Cannot Do 37
Conclusion 39

Introduction

Before you say anything let me answer your questions on "dirty tricks" right in the beginning. Although the title states "Dirty Tricks Narcs Play", that does not mean "illegal" tricks. It simply means that narcotic officers and special agents have plenty of legal and court supported methods to investigate drug crimes. And if you are ever the subject of a drug investigation, any of these methods or all of them will be employed upon you.

You also may wonder why I wrote this book about investigative tricks. Mostly it is because of information sharing. Narcotic investigators can use the information in this book if they don't know it yet and anyone under suspicion can be aware of the methods too. The intent of the book is entertainment so you can compare that which happens on TV to what really happens on the street.

Another reason I thought of writing this book is for the sake of the innocent being trapped into a web of inconsistencies if ever questioned by police and to also help others be aware of tactics that may have them waive or ignore their civil rights. Believe me when I say, you don't want to give up your rights. Ever. Even if you are guilty as sin, keep your rights and make the police do their job.

For everyone else (that is not involved in drugs or police work), you will find this book to be entertaining, enlightening, and at times, a bit frightening in how law enforcement is able to work up the ladder to identify as many people as possible who may be involved in the drug trade as a dealer or user.

As far as legal advice, I have none to give you. This book is strictly for entertainment purposes for those that wonder how drug dealers and narcs operate in the world. It is not a guide on how to defeat the system. Eventually, everyone gets caught, so my only advice is to stay crime free!

Chapter 1 - First Things First

My opinion on drug use doesn't matter. Your opinion doesn't matter either. The only thing that matters is the law. You can fight to change it, but the law is the law.

I say this because no matter how much a user of any drug screams that any or all drugs should be legalized, unless the law is changed, all the arguing doesn't matter. This book keeps opinions of drug use out of the book.

As far as drug dealing, by law, just about every drug user is a drug dealer. Drug dealing is distributing drugs to another. Ever passed a joint? You just distributed drugs. Ever buy a joint? You just involved yourself in a conspiracy to traffic in drugs. Get the point?

Next thing. If you think that knowing the tactics narcotics officers use will help you, don't worry. Eventually, one of the tactics will work and you'll be busted. If you are dealing now and not busted yet, you might want to consider getting out while the getting is good.

Narcotic Officers, Special Agents, and Informants

To keep things simple and organized, let's clarify a few words.

Narcs – typically, this refers to narcotic officers. Narcotic officers can be city cops, county deputies, or state police/troopers. DEA

Special Agents are also known as narcs, but they are "federal" whereas the others (city, county, state) are considered "local" cops.

Narcs spend their days being assigned cases from their agency for every crime under the sun, from prescription forgery to kids with marijuana to crack cocaine found on a street arrest. They also work cases as undercover officers and support their local task force. Narcs have many street level contacts with informants and know the local street dealers. They rarely interact or even know who the bigger drug dealers are, other than what they may hear rumors of. Their goal is to quickly bust a street dealer and move on to the next case. Their cases may last a few hours or few weeks.

Special Agents – Typically, these are the federal law enforcement officers, but some states also have local officers with a job title of special agent. In this book, special agent refers to the actual federal agents. Later, you will see why this is a very important distinction.

Special Agents don't usually work the streets like narcs. They are generally aware of the bigger drug dealers but not the street level dealers. Most will not leave their office and they rely heavily upon local narcs to feed them information and informants. Once they have a case, their goal is to drag it out as long as possible to catch as many dealers as possible. This can take years!

Informants – Informants are also known to be called narcs, but in this book, we are keeping narcs separate from informants. Informants are persons that 'inform' on others. Criminals usually refer to informants as rats or snitches. Informants give information to law enforcement for many reasons. Police reports generally list informants as CI for confidential informant. We'll get into more about informants in detail later.

Cooperating Witness – Cooperating witnesses (CW) are sometimes informants and other times, they may be innocent persons with information to give to law enforcement. A cooperating defendant (CD) is an informant…

Anonymous complainant – Anonymous complaints are many times jilted lovers, victims of a drug deal gone bad, or a concerned citizen. Sometimes, an anonymous complaint is not so anonymous as the narcs may want to hide the actual name of a witness.

Those are the players in the drug enforcement game. Now to get started!

Chapter 2 – Drug Crimes in Brief

This is a quick list of drug crimes, not to educate you in the specifics of intent, knowledge, or sentencing, but to give you an overview of the different charges and seriousness of the crimes.

Possession – *this is merely holding drugs on your person, home, or vehicle. You don't have to be selling it or using it. Just possessing it somehow. BUT, if you have a lot of drugs and/or paraphernalia like a scale to weigh drugs, you could be suspected of intending to distribute the drugs. That is a more serious charge than merely possessing drugs.*

Possession with Intent to Distribute – *If you intended to sell drugs, no matter the amount, this is your charge. It's pretty serious due to the sentencing you can receive.*

Drug Manufacturing – *This is another serious charge if you manufacture drugs, which includes growing marijuana.*

Money Laundering – *If you sell drugs, you are usually doing this too. It's an additional charge. Bought a car with drug money? That's money laundering.*

Homicide with drugs – *also known as a "hot shot" where someone was provided drugs and died from the drugs. This is a very serious charge, obviously.*

Federal versus Local Charges – *this is the first thing to consider when facing any charges. Federal charges can mean severe sentences in federal prison, no matter the type of drug charge, the sentencing is most always more stiff than a local or state level charge.*

Types of drugs – *the type of drug someone is arrested with (buying, selling, manufacturing, transporting, etc..) affects the type of charge and sentencing, as does the amount. For example, if a person cooks a pound of meth and sells it, he can face extremely strict sentencing standards. Conversely, if someone grows five marijuana plants in a closet for personal use, the jail time is nothing close to the guy that is busted with a pound of meth.*

The other factor to consider about charges is this tactic called "stacking charges". This is where the suspect is charged with everything including the kitchen sink, in hopes of copping a guilty plea in exchange for dropping some of the charges. Some judges see through this, but not all.

The number of charges can be extreme depending on the case. If both cocaine and marijuana are seized during an arrest, that is two separate charges with separate sentencing guidelines. Add money laundering for a car or flat screen TV that was purchased and the number of charges just jumped to three. Add failure to report income for taxes and the IRS can get involved with another crime.

With this short section on charges, anyone can easily see why jails are packed with drug crimes. Suspects cannot fight all charges and choose to plea to a lesser charge and lesser time in jail rather than risk decades in prison, even if their case is weak.

Chapter 3 – The First Rung of the Ladder

All cases have to start somewhere. Rarely does a major drug case drop in a narcs lap. It does happen on occasion, but usually, if the narc doesn't do much work, he isn't going to be doing many cases. Let's go through some examples of how cases typically begin. This is important to know as you can see how a cartel is taken down based on the first rung of the ladder; the drug user arrested for possession.

Dirty Trick #1 – Threaten the drug user

By threats, I do not mean threats of bodily harm. When a drug user (ie…addict) has been arrested, he has many reasons to want to get out of his jam. If he is a heroin addict, withdrawals will start about the time he is booked and placed into his cell. His court arraignment may be in a day or two, and then he may be in jail for a few days more. That is a long time to suffer withdrawals.

If he is an upstanding citizen with a job and family, going to jail will have a very negative impact on his life. He certainly wants to avoid the stigma of being a drug convict.

Both of these cases are prime meat to develop into an informant, especially if this is the first arrest or first contact with the police. Even the most inexperienced narc can turn these guys into informants. Any drug dealer that has a customer fitting these descriptions is also ripe to be caught in a covert drug operation.

So, the threats are real when a narc tells either of these guys that he will spend time in jail, go to court, probably get convicted, and sentenced to jail. The narc can simply show the penal code that exactly states possession of a drug equates to a year or more in jail and a thousand dollar or more fine. How much more does the narc have to do? Not much.

Dirty Trick #2 – Promise the World

When a narc promises the world to these guys, he is only promising to either lessen the charge or completely drop it. WHAT!?! Drop the charges? Yes, that is right. Become an informant at this level and you can have your entire case dropped. No conviction, no record. All you have to do is turn someone else in. It's an easy promise and works well. It's also easy for the narc to close the case on a drug user and open a new case on a drug dealer.

Narcs know that immediately after an arrest, the arrestee is ripe to be turned into an informant. Stress is high, fear of the unknown is extreme, and anything sounds better than going to jail. Plus, they may even offer to pay you if you do a good job. Trust me, they will say something that entices you to at least think about it, but they will not tell you all the negative points of being an informant. You will not be a cop, nor have police protection. You will be on your own setting up people for the cops.

How to beat Dirty Trick # 1 and Dirty Trick #2

If the drug addict or drug user was arrested for simple possession of a user amount of drugs, the best counter-defense is to ask for an attorney and not cooperate. If the user cooperates, the rest of his life will consist of living in fear of any drug dealer he turns in. If he asks for a lawyer, he can also ask for leniency as a drug addict, not a drug dealer. Remember, once a rat, always a rat. Think twice before falling for the threats and promises.

What happens if you cooperate?

This is when it will get scary. You most likely will have to wear a body wire and you don't want to get caught wearing one of those. You will most certainly have to call your drug dealer and order drugs. The point is to set up your dealer so he is arrested. No matter what the narcs tell you, they are going to arrest your dealer. It may be that day or the next week, but eventually, they will arrest him.

The thing you have to worry about is being disclosed as the informant. Your drug dealer will be mad and any other dealer is not going to want to be around you. More importantly, your safety in doing a drug deal under the 'protection' of the police isn't much protection at all. They will give you marked money, watch you go into the dealer's house or car and wait for you to come out with drugs. If you have a problem inside, you are on your own unless the narcs decide to rescue you, that is, if they hear you calling for help.

Potentially, your dealer will be arrested on the spot, right in front of you. No promise of being kept confidential by the narcs will hold water to your dealer. You will be burned.

The methods you will be used as an informant are discussed in another chapter, but be aware that as an informant, you are less human than anyone else in the eyes of a narc. Even to a narc, you are rat. It is what it is and totally your decision as to what you want to do. You can never go wrong asking for a lawyer.

Now, if you do cooperate, and everything goes as planned, you might be home without a worry in the world. Your dealer gets arrested and is made into an informant. You are no longer needed to 'work off your beef' and can relax. But, let's say your dealer doesn't cooperate and goes to trial. Your life will have just taken a turn for the worst. You will be needed for trial. Your identity might be disclosed (as if your dealer didn't know anyway). Your role as an informant might just make the Internet or local news. This is all out of your hands. This is the chance you take when you become an informant. If a narc promises to keep your name confidential, all it takes is a judge to order your name to be disclosed.

Chapter 4 – Informant Development

I covered a little about developing an informant in the previous chapter. This chapter goes more into the nitty gritty of developing an informant. While you read this, consider what the narcs are saying while you sit in a cell waiting for them to talk to you.

They will plan on you "folding like a cheap card table", "rolling like a donut", and "turning into a snitch on mitch". They will play good cop-bad cop, make promises and threats, and wait for you to stop crying so you can agree to be their informant.

Even a seasoned drug dealer will fall prey to Dirty Trick # 1 and Dirty Trick #2 if the timing is right. But if not, there are a few more tricks up their sleeves.

Dirty Trick # 3 – Play to emotions

Perhaps you are mad at your significant other (or ex), your dealer (because you owe lots of money), or you want to close down a competitor. Narcs will use your anger in their favor because now you can get even and set these people up. Not only do you get off your charges, but you can get even using the police. How about that deal?

The problem is that your emotions change. Mad today is forgiven tomorrow. When this tactic is used, it is used quickly because narcs know this emotion is usually short-lived. You will be setting someone up tonight and by tomorrow, you will regret it.

Another play on emotions is for you to **"do the right thing"** and turn in your dealer. Besides, it was your dealer's fault that you use drugs or sell drugs. You are only selling to make ends meet, so why should you go to jail. Again, doing the right thing may or may not be turning in someone else. For the narcs, it doesn't matter which reason you turn someone it, just that you do.

How do defend against Dirty Trick #3

Keep your emotions in check. Take a breather. Talk to a lawyer. Don't do anything right now until you can think about the consequences. The narcs will tell you it is now or never, but 99% of the time, they will wait. If a narc does tell you that it is now or never and means it that may be in your best interest anyway. Any narc that is so rushed to turn you into fodder for their next case might not be the narc you want to talk with.

Dirty Trick #4 – Narcs promise to tell everyone you a rat

A common trick is releasing an arrestee and telling him that everyone will think he is a rat. Then, he will be no longer able to buy drugs and dealers will want to harm him. If they did this, they would be putting your life in danger. But, they also know that when dealers see arrestees get out of jail after a few hours or days without charges, something is not right.

How do defend against Dirty Trick #4

Do not let anyone lead you to believe your life is in danger unless they are threatening to actually do that. Clarify that if your life is in danger because of their actions, perhaps they should consider seeking legal protection if something happens to you. Tell your attorney that you are being played and your life risked. Remember also that, every person arrested is eventually released, at least for non-violent crimes. Charges are rarely filed immediately as jails are full and cops are too busy to keep up with paperwork. Getting out of jail is nothing other than getting out and waiting for your court date if it ever comes.

Dirty Trick #5 – Help us to help you

If you have a drug addiction problem, you need professional help. A narcotics officer is not professional help. You will be told that burning your dealer is the first step to your recovery. Do the right thing and take that first step to burn your dealer. This way, you will not be able to buy drugs anymore.

How do defend against Dirty Trick #5

Do not believe for an instant that turning in your dealer will cure your addition or even put you on the road to recovery. You need treatment, not work as an informant. Ask the judge for treatment.

Don't ask the narc for treatment. He only wants to arrest people. Treatment wants you not to be arrested. As much as you may feel this will help your addiction, trust me, it won't do a thing for it.

Dirty Trick #6 – They let you go without saying anything

If you refuse to be an informant or ask to speak to an attorney, they most likely will just release you pending charges. Usually, they will also be mad that you didn't cooperate. Be prepared to be watched. Be prepared that someone may try to set you up. You see, if you didn't cooperate with one charge, stacking more charges on you will do the trick.

Narcs will use one informant to buy from a person for the sole reason to make a new informant, or to make a point. This happens and it can happen to you. Informants can be anyone, even your closest friend.

How do defend against Dirty Trick #6

Don't buy or sell drugs after you are released. If you do, stand by for getting caught. You just made the list of who the narcs want to watch and if they have nothing better to do, you are it. Go to treatment, follow whatever treatment says, and talk to your lawyer.

Dirty Trick #7 – You better talk before your friend does...

When more than one person has been arrested, you will be given the "opportunity" to turn in your friend before your friend turns you in. Guess what. Your friend is being given the same talk. This tactic works wonders because you just don't know what your friend is going to say. It might not even a friend, but someone you just met. Worse still, this other person can make up anything and pin all the blame on you. You could be named the kingpin! Like I said, this tactic works wonders.

How do defend against Dirty Trick #7

You better know your friends before this happens. You should know if you can trust your friends and they should know if you can be trusted. If you are barely known to the other person, you can prepare yourself of the other guy blaming you for everything. Again, a lawyer is a wonderful thing because asking for a lawyer means the police can't ask you any more questions. Maybe if everyone did that....

Given these tactics, informants are developed every day of every year in every state. It is the way it works. Hopefully, you asked for an attorney and work toward treatment rather than becoming a "rat". Although I have managed dozens of informants, I've always believed that taking responsibility is important, not blaming someone else.

Dirty Trick #8 – Screaming, yelling and name calling...

Unless you have been to military basic training, being screamed and yelled at by someone in authority is intimidating. It is so intimidating for some that agreeing to anything just to make it stop is a common result. Being denigrated, demeaned, and insulted is a means to an end of developing an informant. No, it's not proper and it is dehumanizing, but it works.

How to defend against Dirty Trick #8

Don't take it personally. The narc is usually out of control at this point. This may also be the last ditch effort to turn you, so be patient, realize that the yelling will eventually be over, and remember the names you were called. You'll need to recite them to your attorney later. Unless you are being physically harmed, all the yelling in the world isn't going to do much to you.

Chapter 5 – Surveillance Tactics

There are lots of ways to conduct surveillance on someone. Actually, there are more ways than you can imagine. Some are sneaky and others are plainly visible.

Dirty Trick #9 – Following you around

This is the most common tactic. Sometimes narcs want you to know you are being followed to cause frustration for you. Most times, they want to catch you in the act of buying or selling drugs, and to identify everyone you know. A lot of intelligence can be gained simply following someone around for a period of time.

Airplanes are vehicle tool of choice, but rare unless (1) the suspect is a major dealer and (2) there is an airplane to use. Drones are popular in the military, but in police work, they have not yet made into mainstream surveillance. That day may come, but it's not here yet.

How to defend against Dirty Trick #9

There isn't much to can do to prevent being followed, other than trying to lose those who follow you. You'll have to employ 'counter-surveillance' driving. This simply means you drive in circles, backtrack often, stop in parking lots for a few minutes and leave, enter stores and exit, use covered parking garages, and ride buses. Don't be routine, make it difficult for the narcs to plan to follow you.

If you speed or violate traffic laws, you stand to be pulled over and cited by the people you are trying to avoid, just because they may want to give you reasons to cooperate in hopes of less attention they give to you.

Dirty Trick #10 – Video cameras pointed at your home or work

Unless the narcs come onto your property, you'll have to live with being video recorded. This is one of those methods that make surveillance really easy since all that needs to be done is replace batteries and tapes on a regular basis.

How to defend against Dirty Trick #10

Remember that your privacy is INSIDE your home, not at work, not in your car, not while shopping. If you can see the cameras, you can always make it a little more difficult by moving large objects on your property to block the view, like tall plants. But also remember that you most likely will not even know the cameras are there. For that reason alone, don't forget that your privacy is INSIDE your home, so close your curtains.

Dirty Trick #11 – Phone toll and cell tower analysis

Again, this is a method that is labor free for narcs. All a narc needs is to send a request to obtain your cell phone records and cell tower hits. From there, everyone you called and everyone that called you is listed on a sheet of paper with dates, times, and numbers. Cell tower records show your location. With both records, narcs can see who you called and an approximant location of where you were during the calls. They won't have the content of your conversations, but this is the next best thing.

How to defend against Dirty Trick #11

Don't use your phone. Use a prepaid phone, commonly called burners, throwaway phones, or cold phones. Replace the phone every month. This makes it harder to create a visual depiction of all your contacts, but not impossible since they can just as easily obtain records from the people you call.

Dirty Trick #12 – Internet access

Yes, narcs can get records on your Internet activity. Every website you have visited and the words you used to search on the Internet. For your emails, a search warrant is needed, but currently, the metadata (the receiver, sender, and dates) of emails is fair game. Be careful to whom you email because an innocent email can be considered suspicious depending upon who it is you email.

How to defend against Dirty Trick #12

Your Internet Service Provider (ISP) will provide all Internet records at law enforcement's request for the payor (subscriber) of the account. This applies to every computer in your home, so if you have anyone in your home committing crimes online, you should get them out of your home before you get blamed. Nothing online is safe, especially if spyware or keyloggers are placed on your computer by cops. Usually, it takes a very big case for this to happen, but it is possible.

Dirty Trick #14 – Using your neighbors as spy agents

This is a really dirty trick. Narcs will sometimes contact your neighbors, imply you are a criminal, and ask that they keep track of you and your visitors. Your neighbors may not tell you, but they might start acting different around you.

How to defend against Dirty Trick #14

Know your neighbors. Make sure they know you as a good guy, not a criminal. If you notice anything suspicious, such as your neighbor writing down license plates of your visitors, then you can assume they may be a narc's spy. As with anything, don't tell anyone about personal and private business. That includes your neighbors.

Dirty Trick #15 – Public travels

In many cities, there are cameras everywhere. Red-light cameras, speeding cameras, security cameras, and personal cameras on cell phones. The public cameras (red-light, etc...) snap photos of your car, license plate, and driver. These photos are marked with date, time, and location. It is a simple request for a city narc to ask the city for all records of your car's travels.

How to defend against Dirty Trick #15

Remember that wherever you drive, you have probably been recorded by some camera at some point. You just never know where or when. This is important to know as it relates to Dirty Trick #16.

Dirty Trick #16 – Obstruction of justice

If you are questioned by law enforcement, there are worse things that confessing a crime. The one thing worse: lying. The thing about lying is that if the police can't get you for a crime that they are investigating, they can trick you into painting yourself into a corner and charge you for obstruction of justice (lying).

How to defend against Dirty Trick #16

Some easy lies are those that the narcs can prove without dispute. For example, if you lied about your whereabouts and the police have a photo of you in your car that disproves your statement, you might be charged for obstruction.

The defense to Dirty Trick #16 is the same as several others: Talk to your lawyer, not the police, even if you are completely and absolutely innocent. Actually, especially if you are innocent, don't talk to the police. Like I said, an innocent person can innocently "lie" about a small fact by omission and have that considered to be the crime of obstruction.

Chapter 6 – Drug Operations

Dirty Trick #17 – Buy Walks

A buy-walk is when the police buy drugs from a drug dealer and don't arrest the dealer. The entire deal is made to look like a normal drug deal using an undercover officer or informant. The goal is to identify the dealer, his home, his other buyers, his suppliers, and his assets. It is also used to build trust with small deals in order to buy larger amounts of drugs or be introduced to a bigger drug dealer.

How to defend against Dirty Trick #17

Don't sell drugs. That solves this problem. But if you happen to provide user amounts of drugs to "friends", be aware that your "friend" could be a new informant of the police. So, don't even give drugs to your friends.

Dirty Trick #18 – Buy Busts

This is the same as the buy-walk, except that after the deal is done, an arrest is made. Usually it is made on the spot, other times it may be made once the dealer leaves and he is arrested elsewhere. As soon as the deal is done, the arrest is made through speed, shock, and surprise. You won't see it coming or know what happened until it is all over.

How to defend against Dirty Trick #18

See "How to defend against Dirty Trick #17".

Dirty Trick #19 – Drug or money flashes

If for some reason someone talks to you about a drug deal, in that he wants you to sell drugs or buy drugs, you will eventually see a "flash" of whatever the person wants to give you. Narcs will flash dealers a large amount of cash for the purpose of enticing a dealer to sell to them. Or they may flash drugs (seized from a different case) and entice you to purchase the drugs. Buying or selling is a crime and if you happen to be surprised with a wad of cash or bag of drugs, consider that you may be getting set up.

How to defend against Dirty Trick #19

See "How to defend against Dirty Trick #17".

Dirty Trick #20 - Introductions

Similar to the flash, an introduction is a narc or informant at a narc's direction, asking you to "hook them up" to a dealer. By asking you to join in setting up a deal, you become part of the deal and another stat to be jotted in the narc's case for arrests.

How to defend against Dirty Trick #20

Don't do it. "Hooking" someone up to a drug deal makes you a conspirator, and part of the crime. Don't do it. See "How to defend against Dirty Trick #17".

Dirty Trick #21 – Search warrants and sneak and peaks

By the time narcs have a search warrant, they have you dead to rights. Search warrants are only given when there is probable cause (meaning enough evidence to arrest). When the knock comes, open the door and comply. The only times you wont know about a search warrant is when you have been served with a 'sneak and peek' warrant. In this type of warrant, the narcs will quietly enter your home or car when you are not around, search it or plant listening devices) and leave without giving notice to you until after their investigation is over. GPS Devices are placed in this manner too (see Dirty Trick #22).

How to defend against Dirty Trick #21

You can't defend against a warrant, other than do not do anything that will have the police write a search warrant for you or your home. For the sneak and peek warrant, you can barricade your home to reduce bugs being planted, but even then, there is usually a around everything.

Dirty Trick #22 – Wiretaps and recordings

One of the best types of evidence is that of the suspect's spoken word. It's solid and clear. Law enforcement can tap your phone almost as easy as flipping a switch. But like a search warrant, they need probable cause and court approval to tap your phone. If your phone is tapped, they already have you. Worse still, if you happen to call a phone of someone you know and their phone is tapped; your conversation will be recorded. You could have been invisible to the police but with that phone call, be placed to the top of the chart as a target.

Conversely, if an undercover narc or informant talks to you on the phone, they can record that phone call with the consent of the undercover or informant. Almost every state allows this without any paperwork other than an administrative form to be filled out by the narc. Probable cause is not needed, so it is fast, easy, and unpredictable.

How to defend against Dirty Trick #22

You can't against your calls being recorded. You can only not commit crimes or incriminate yourself on the phone. That includes calling your lawyer on the phone. Those calls are protected, even if you are being recorded by the police on the call, but can you really trust that the police will not use information they happen to hear when you were talking to your attorney? Technically, they are to stop listening once they determine you are speaking with your lawyer, but....

Dirty Trick #23 – Secret information

There are agencies in the federal government that obtain information on citizens and criminals on a 24/7 basis through all the techniques in this book. Many of the methods are closely guarded secrets, such as wiretaps or major case investigations that are ongoing.

When any of these agencies come across information on a suspected criminal because of a phone call or anonymous tip or surveillance, they will pass the information to another agency. The receiving agency promises not to disclose the source of the information and must create a new case. Their new case starts with confirming the anonymous/secret information and starting fresh.

Once this is done, the new agency can makes arrests, serve warrants, and seize property based SOLELY on the information they obtained. HOWEVER, the original source of the information was from a secret agency, such as the DEA's Special Operations Division or the CIA or even the NSA.

How to defend against Dirty Trick #23

You can't prevent the information from being shared. If you called a wiretapped phone and your information is passed to another agency and that is just the way it works. You will now have a case against you when you didn't before.

But, if you go to trial, make sure your attorney deposes (questions) all involved officers and narcs in your case. Your attorney needs to ask, "When was the first time you suspected my client of criminal activity?". The officer has a choice to lie and state his report reflects the answer, or he will tell the truth and say a secret agency gave the information.

Technically, the officer must tell the truth, especially in court, even if it compromises the investigation and secret unit that obtained the information. Once that happens, your attorney can demand discovery (right to see the other information) for trial and a whole bucket of worms gets opened. If the officer lies in court or in the deposition, and this is found out later, then the officer that arrested you can be charged for perjury. You get out of jail, he goes in.

Chapter 7 – Consent searches

This chapter goes more into a very interesting subject where narcs either don't want to apply for a search warrant or they just don't have enough evidence. Sometimes, they are just plain lazy.

Dirty Trick #24 – Consent searches

When the police come knocking at your door, they are either going to bust it open because they have a search warrant or they want you to let them in without a warrant. If a narc asks you to search your home and you let him in, you just gave up your protection against search and seizure. This is the fastest method to search a home or car or person by police. They just have to ask and you have to give your consent. Anything and everything they find is fair game to use against you in criminal charges. Within 30 seconds, you can have a full search of your home started just by opening the door and talking.

How to defend against Dirty Trick #24

Don't consent to a search. Ever. Even if you have nothing to hide, don't consent. You just don't know what you have that could be considered illegal or maybe left by your friends. Don't do it. As a matter of fact, don't even open the door unless the narcs have a search warrant. Go back to watching tv. They will go away eventually. They won't be happy, but you won't have your home trashed and risk going to jail for something you may have forgotten about.

When you are being asked for your consent, the manner of the asking leads you to agree in waiving your protections against being searched. Questions like, "You don't have any drugs or guns in your car, do you?" lead you to immediately say "no" and then you feel like you have to prove it by saying, "go ahead and check". Just don't do it. You don't have to answer any questions or let anyone search your home or car without a search warrant.

The longer you talk with any experienced narc, the more risk you will have of digging yourself in a hole and end up in cuffs when all you had to do was not talk in the first place.

Make the police do their job and get a warrant if they have evidence. If you are not doing anything illegal, you have nothing to worry about anyway, so why let the police trample all over your home and try to find something. If they had evidence on you, they wouldn't be asking.

Chapter 8 – Moving Up the Ladder

Most of what I've covered is focused on the end user of a drug. Experienced narcs know that even a lowly marijuana user can find drug dealers that sell crack or heroin. So, many narcs will arrest anyone for drugs, even for the smallest amount, just for the chance of turning a new informant into the wild to find bigger fish.

That is the goal of all narcs. They keep going until;

1. They reach the farthest distance they want to travel or the end of their jurisdiction.

2. They arrest the 'main dealer' in their area.

3. Someone refuses to inform on others and the case ends there.

4. Or they stop whenever they want.

You are just a single part of this ladder to be stepped on. Many times, when a local narc reaches the end of his case due to resources or distance, he may pass it on to a federal agency to follow up. This is how bigger dealers get nailed, through the initial start of the first arrestee that starts the upward chain of investigative events.

And don't forget. There is a record of you being an informant if you so choose to do so. Promises of being confidential are just promises. A judge can overrule a narc to disclose your name. Even if you are promised confidentiality, if something changes in the case, like someone getting killed, your promises of being confidential may be thrown out the window.

As far as witness protection goes, don't get your hopes up. A local narc's department does not have the money for witness protection, nor do they have the urge to provide protection. If anything, they will pass that on to a federal agency. But consider, if you are buying dime bags or rocks of crack for $50 as an informant, your chances of getting witness protection is about as good as winning the lottery, or worse. Witness protection requires a whole lot more than a drug dealer being mad at you.

As I mentioned, you will be stepped on as part of the ladder, and as your best buddy narc has had his use of you, he will move on to someone else. Your "friendship" was only a means to gain your cooperation. Don't expect to be hanging out him because almost all narcs consider informants to be worse than the criminals they inform on. It is dehumanizing, but it is also the way it is.

Chapter 9 – Cash and Asset Seizures

The most important goal for narcotic law enforcement is different, depending upon who you are.

For the general public, the most important goal is arresting drug dealers.

For narcs, the most important goal is seizing cash and assets. The second most important is arresting drug dealers.

Dirty Trick #25 – Asset Forfeiture

When the police come knocking at your door, they are either going to bust Most narcs act as if the money they seize will be deposited into their personal accounts as a bonus. For every car, every house, and every dollar, they get an 'attaboy' from their boss. Their boss takes the stats of seizures to the Chief or Sheriff, who then thinks about how to spend this free money. At this point, everyone in the chain has just become addicted to cash and asset seizures and consider arrests secondary.

There are more than a few cases where a suspect has been arrested and had his car and cash seized, only to be let go with no charges. The arrestee is happy he is not in jail and the police are happy they have money to spend on equipment and training. Plus, they get a pat on the back for taking away a drug dealer's stuff.

This invariably leads narcs to seizing everything, even things they have no right to seize. Justice is not being served when this happens and the narc unit becomes a revenue generating unit, not a drug enforcement unit. This happens. A lot.

How to defend against Dirty Trick #25

Don't commit any crimes and your property can't be legally seized. Otherwise, anything in your name that is suspected to have been purchased with proceeds of drug crimes can be seized. That includes your cars, house, watch, computer, TV, anything, and everything. The more you have, the more they can take.

If you have made any large purchases, especially with cash, be prepared to keep documentation as to the source of that cash. That will be the only proof you have to show your property was legally gained with legal money. Otherwise, you most likely will lose it and you don't even have to be charged with a crime. Remember; keep documentation of your income because in the case of asset of forfeiture, the burden of legal ownership is on YOU. Yes, this is America.

Chapter 10 – They Lie, But You Can't

I touched briefly about telling the truth or face obstruction of justice charges. That rule doesn't apply to narcs unless they are testifying or writing reports. They can lie lie lie to you. They can tell you that there is a ton of evidence against you, that your friends and neighbors turned you in, and that you will spend eternity in prison.

You, on the other hand, better not even tell a white lie (don't say anything!) because if you do, that is a criminal charge.

What do the courts say on this? They approve. So, telling the court that the narc lied to you means nothing because the court will say, "so what."

Chapter 11 – Some Things Narcs Cannot Do

I talked a lot about what narcs can do in an investigation, but there are also many things they cannot do. Some of these things are;

1. **Beat informants** – *unless you start it, they can't just beat you because they want. They can only protect themselves from you.*

2. **Beat suspects** – *unless you start it, they can't just beat you because they want. They can only protect themselves from you.*

3. **Steal property** – *this includes your personal property during a search warrant, but of course, they can seize property.*

4. **Lie in court or reports** – *but they can lie to you.*

5. **Have sex with informants or suspects** – *can't do this, ever, as it ruins the case.*

6. **Do drugs (with anyone)** – *but they can if someone puts a gun to their head if it means avoiding getting killed.*

7. **Commit crimes** – *but they commit some crimes if approved by their agency or a court to show proof of being a criminal when undercover.*

You can see that some things they can do, others they can do if certain situations apply, and some things they just can't do. Every citizen should be aware of the legal authority and legal constraints of law enforcement, especially narcs, since it may seem they are overreaching when they may be within their legal rights. Other times, you may not know they overreached their authority if you don't know the constraints or your legal rights.

Conclusion

I wrote this book to be entertaining and as a glimpse into the world of narcotic investigations. Nothing I gave is top secret, confidential, proprietary, or even a closely guarded secret. Everything is not only public records (court cases, reports), but also all over the Internet in one place or a dozen others.

My intention is not for drug dealers to get away with dealing drugs, or for drug users to be able to sustain their habit. It is rather to help you, the reader understand that mistakes can be made in law enforcement that can directly affect you.

Also, there is nothing in this book that will increase drug use or sales, nor decrease drug use or sales. But one thing is for sure, you are now more educated than you were before reading this book. The next time you watch a police drama on television, you'll be able to point out the Hollywood hype from the real-life narcs. Now that's entertainment.

If you are reading this book in order to learn how to be a drug dealer or a better drug dealer, you got the wrong book.

www.ingramcontent.com/pod-product-compliance
Lightning Source LLC
Chambersburg PA
CBHW070720180526
45167CB00004B/1559